LIZ NIVEN is a Scottish based poet an ~~~~~~~~~~~~~~~~~~~~~~~
Scots. She has been a teacher, a Scots ~~~~~~~~~~~~~~~~~~~~~~~
and a schools' Cultural Co-ordinato ~~~~~~~~~~~~~~~~~~~~~~~
variety of art forms to produce books, pnotographic cards and public
art text-based installations. She has written and edited a wide range
of award-winning language resources for the renaissance of the Scots
Language in education and the community. Editorial work includes
annual volumes of new writing from the Association of Scottish
Literary Studies. She delivers creative writing workshops for Arts
bodies including the Scottish Poetry Library, London Poetry Society,
National Galleries of Scotland and Scottish Natural Heritage. She is
one of Scotland's most popular school poetry facilitators and has
worked on projects with young people to put poetry into unusual
locations. These include gardens, classrooms and the fabric of school
buildings. She has been invited to participate in poetry readings and
Festivals including Edinburgh Book Festival, StAnza, Wigtown, N.
Ireland, Lithuania, Slovakia, Finland and China.

Other books by Liz Niven

Poetry

Past Presents (Akros)
Cree Lines (DGAA/Watergaw)
A Drunk Wumman Sittin oan a Thistle (Markings)
Stravaigin (Canongate & Luath)
Burning Whins (Luath)
Cracked Ice (Roncadora)

Plays

Killing Time (Spotlight Productions)
A Play Aboot Ninian (D&G.Educ.Dept/Watergaw)

Educational

Haud Yer Tongue (Channel 4)
Turnstones 1 (Co-ed. Hodder &Stoughton)
The Kist/A Chiste (Co-ed. SCCC/Nelson Blackie)
Solway Stills (Co-ed.D&G.Educ.Dept)
The Sound of our Voices (Co-ed.D&G.Libraries)
Doadies Boadie (SLRC)
The Scots language: Its Place in Education (Watergaw)
Scots Language in Education in Scotland: Mercator (EBLUL, Netherlands)
Its a Braw Brew (Co-ed.Watergaw)

Editorial

A Bucket of Frogs (ASLS)
The Dynamics of Balsa (ASLS)
In the Event of Fire (ASLS)

The Shard Box

LIZ NIVEN

Alistair
guid tge see
ye again!
Liz Niven

Luath Press Limited

EDINBURGH

www.luath.co.uk

First published 2010

ISBN 978-1-906817-62-6

The publisher acknowledges subsidy from

 Scottish
Arts Council

towards the publication of this book.

The paper used in this book is recyclable. It is made from
low chlorine pulps produced in a low energy, low emissions
manner from renewable forests.

Printed and bound by
Bell & Bain Ltd., Glasgow

Typeset in 10.5pt Sabon by
3btype.com

The author's right to be identified as author of this book under the
Copyright, Designs and Patents Acts 1988 has been asserted.

© Liz Niven 2010

For family and friends, West and East

Acknowledgements

I'd like to thank;

my family at home and in China especially Jenny and David in Beijing

Alex Pearson, Pete Goff and staff at The Bookworms in Beijing, Suzhou and Chengdu and Fernando Reyes Matta, the Chilean Ambassador in Beijing for accommodation and sponsorship

Janet Paisley, Brian Whittingham, Valentina Bold and Tom Pow

the Scottish Arts Council for two travel grants awarded to support my visits.

Some of the poems in *The Shard Box* have appeared or been broadcast in:

The Herald, Chapman, Lallans, Chuckies fir the Cairn, Cracked Ice, Markings, Poetry Scotland, In the Margins, Opium Magazine, New York, Radio Beijing, Chinese Radio International and BBC *World Service*. 'Tian'anmen kites' and 'Efter ye cam back fae Malawi' were award winners in the McCash poetry prize.

Contents

Moon Gate

Now we are
   gazing at the Moon Gate.
      Its base semi-circles
         The ground.
            Not reaching to earth
               It's suspended in stone.
               A stone moon.
                  A solid hoop to jump through.
                  A wedding ring
                    for a giant.
                      Mao said women hold
                    up half the sky,
                     here skilled stonemen bring the moon
                  down to earth.
            Half a globe away
          we build our gates in a western fashion,
      all the way to ground level.
     The Moon Gate's a zero here.
   Under the same moon
  we lift and lay shared earth.
 Let's consider the Moon Gate,
we must go through it together.

Maybe made in China

Maybe someone is building a road
hoping a car will lessen their load

Maybe someone cooks noodles in a pot
glad for a moment's independent thought

Maybe Falun Gong won't be persecuted
Petty thieves not be executed

Maybe pollution is being sorted
Baby daughters not aborted

Maybe a new Dalai Lama is born
Tibet freed on a summer's morn

Maybe a writer writes anything he likes
Maybe cars won't force out the bikes

Maybe a journalist is freed from jail
endangered tiger oil no longer for sale

Maybe the hutongs are being rebuilt
repairs also made to houses on stilts

Maybe Tian'anmen Mothers can pray
Christians go to church on Sunday

Maybe Xinjiang Muslims can free
Their people under democracy

Maybe Mao's photo will leave the Square
the Red Army stop gathering there

Maybe a newspaper will say what it thinks
the internet stop restricting its links

Maybe schools will be free to all
doctors and health costs finally fall

Maybe your shoes have labels the same
As your furniture, sports gear, toys and games

'Made in China' clothes much of the West
Maybe check that before voicing protests.

The song of the migrant worker

We're building the ring road round Beijing,
helping support Olympic dreams.
Green beans and noodles twice a day.
Yes, we're building the ring road round Beijing.

Twenty of us in the dormitory.
Family back in Hunan Province wait.
Three hundred yuan a month we send them back.
Yes, we're building the ring road round Beijing.

Beggars shooed off the avenue,
New BMWs every week.
See the new underground opens,
while we're building the ring road round Beijing.

We'll return to our fields when work is done,
back to our peasant farming lives.
But we know now how city people live,
because we're building the ring road round Beijing.

Clean fingernails, leather shoes,
washed clothes every day.
High-heeled girls with mobile phones.
We see them at the ring road round Beijing.

China with so many new roads now.
where they will take us when we're done,
when we finish the ring road round Beijing?
It's nearly finished the ring road round Beijing.

Migrant workers

This flittin fae citie tae citie
A few month here, a few month there.

This isnae a gap year.

Kids haein time oot stravaigin,
ettlin tae meet cool folk
in a hostel faur fae hame.

Budweiser in wan haun,
a chick in the ither.
Hing oot, chill oot, space oot.

This isnae rich weans wi da's credit caird,
A few month maturin braidenin horizons,
Explorin the world afore uni or work.

This is folk fleein fae povertie.
Migrant workers luikin fir income,
twintie tae a dormitorie,
bunk bed if ye're lucky.

Mair Steinbeck than Kerouak.

Machine

The blue box in the Beijing apartment
is a clever conundrum;
it filters, cools and boils water.

CCTV plays in the corner,
our joke to count how long it takes
for Japan to be blamed,
for something, anything, everything;
fishing rights, the weather, the price of oil.

A Nanjing massacre programme
tells us 300,000 were killed in seven weeks.
Our joke's no longer funny.

The next report's a street demonstration,
against 'biased history books'.

It's rare uprisings are permitted,
reported or broadcast.

Bubbles slip to the surface
gurgle in the warm evening heat.

Realisation trickles slowly too.

Outside the city skyline shifts to a blazing red.

The machine rumbles on,
filtering efficiently.

CCTV *is the English Language Chinese Television Channel.*

Stable economy

Trade still rests on the ordinary too.
A man cycling his wares to work.

A bike with a cart upon which
he's piled shiny pottery horses.

At least fifty of various sizes.
Their pointed ears rise out of

the jumble of polythene wrapping,
erect behind the Chinese cyclist.

A grubby white towel
hangs over his handlebars.

His face expressionless,
the horses motionless.

Only the yuan fluctuating wildly.

A teatime conversation

The Ocean People,
> (*that was what they called us, and our allies,*
> *coming in by water*)

brought opium
> (*from our already raped colonies*)

to trade for tea
> (*frowned upon intially by polite Edinburgh society*)

and rhubarb
> (*its effects embarrassed many a gent*)

and silk
> (*for ladies to wear in their lounges when receiving*
> *tea-drinking guests*),

and porcelain
> (*needed to contain the new drink*)

Opium wars ensued
> (*enter the British Lord Macartney*)

humiliations fell on China from the west
> (*addicts by the thousand now in dark corners of*
> *shady hutongs*)

Tea was partaken
> (*by ladies in fine dresses in bright New Town*
> *apartments*)

and Trade discussed.

Compound
for F.R. Matta

I've never lived behind metal gates before
     a criss cross lattice work of sheet steel
in the Embassy street of compounds.

Concrete walls conceal South American interiors
     sunflower yellow, clay pot terracotta
your own charcoal drawings piling upstairs.

How does this greyer city suit you?
     Your love of colour, music, poetry,
stories of pre-ambassadorial careers, film-making with Neruda.

Given my own key, tiny and coded, I return each night,
     nod to the young straight-backed Chinese sentry guard.
A smile cracks through after seven days graft
     till the gates whirr shut upon another eastern trip.

I'm home up the Glen again
     our miniature country with its bonsai parliament,
language variations on an Anglo-Saxon-Celtic theme.
     I pick over photographs, ephemera.
Flesh out bones of memory under chopstick white skies.

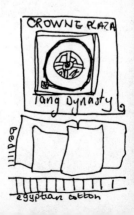

798 Art District

disused factories sprawl across miles
    noodles of empty pipes link overhead
somewhere from another century
    workers voices call over clanking machinery
this must have been a cold workplace
    for blue-overalled citizens
or bosses in their little mao-collared suits

we cross to the gates of 798
    grafitti gazes from walls
sculptures stare down avenues
    of strolling Sunday walking
snack-munching Chinese families

inside shells of factories,
    art has taken residence
Soul Guardians in an Age of Disasters and Calamities
    Or *Accumulations – The Spirit of the East*
we can take our pick of cutting-edge contemporary with an
    Asian slant

sleek black-dressed arts assistants offer wine,
    platters of crackers and sweet biscuits,
Fernando discusses innovative venues,
    residencies, artistic freedom

here now is all exhibition-space
      artists have moved their studios off site
to clapped-out warehouses miles downtown
      798 has become too bourgeois, less bohemian

we stop at a shop stocked with books and prints
      art history west and east, art biographies,
reproductions in cardboard tubes for transporting
      tissue-wrapped carefully as memories

Let's hear whit the dragon's goat tae say

Listen
It's no gonnie be easie this.
If ye think it's a skoosh case ye're wrang.
A've been ettlin tae mak masel heard fir yonks
An naebodie a mean naebodie listens.
A've goat, ma shades, ma ipod, ma Nokia
An a've stoapt spittin fire.
Soon as the taxi boays stoapt gobbin a stoapt.
Solidarity brithers eh?
We need tae work thegither if this kintra's gan oniewhaur.
An damsels. Dinna tak tae me aboot wummen.
Furst aff there's no enough o them.
Mind how it yaised tae be. Boays wir the bees knees.
Needit for the fairmin, liftit heavy stuff.
Shilpit lassies wirnae wantit. Cannae dae the joabs. Dochters
    wir droont.
Mair boather than they wir wirth awbodie said.
An noo thir's no enough o them!
A havenae had a damsel in distress fir years
An onie thit there is his left the kintraside.
Tellin ye they're aw aff tae the Jing,
Meetin whiteys. Makin a fortune. Big joabs.
Thir no likely tae gan oot wi wee reuch an readie fermers boays
  wi stra in thir bunnets, never mind merry them?
Aw naw. Whit a boorach.
Whaur's it gonnie end? That's whit a'm askin.
There'll be a population crisis that's whit. A demographic
    stooshie.

Wan wean policie? Hauf the time it's a nae wean policie.
Aw thae lahdedah citie wummen.
Teeterin aboot wi thir heich heels an perjink wee cocktail frocks.
They're no wantin weans.
Mair lik wantin a dug. Twa dugs.
Bow wow mao.
Wee white Pekinese things
Ye see tham aw ower the Jing,
mincin aboot oan thir wee kiddie oan feet.
No even worth poppin oan a cocktail stick.
Nae eatin in them.
Mind that's aw been chyngin an aw.
Haurdlie onie dug an donkey restaurant onie mair.
The West doesnae like it, they're seyin.
The West doesnae like it?
The West can tak a rin an jump tae itsel
A'll tell you this,
It'll no much maitter soon whit the West wants.
Fowerhunnerandsixtemillion mobile phone yaisers.
Fiftyechtmillion mair nor last year Eh?
An caurs.Jeeso.
Dinna get me stertit oan yon.
Gie's a brek. Ye can come back tae me oan that yin.
A'm awa tae licht up
A need A fag. At least ye can still hiv a fag inside ower here.

23

Blin shaft

A fin a cinema shawin Inglis leid
subtitlt Chinese films.

The plot based on a real life tale:
crooks whae prey oan lanely young fowk,

wheedlin thir wey doon mines,
cheatin managers oot o compensation.

Gin the mine shaft faws in they claim it's
killt thir 'brither'.

Set amangst a dreich teuch backgrun,
hard leevin pair fowk

sennin siller back hame
tae faimiles fae a cluster

o widden shacks at the fuit o
slopin slag covert bens in China's noreast.

The cinema's that bonnie.
Ceilin paintit tradeetional

reid an blae squerrs fillt wi
picters o flooers, beasts, burds,

cloods an lifts an heich bens.
Ma een muives atween sub-titles,

screen tae ceilin an back again.
Like this kintra, it's a conundrum

A cannae crack or comprehend.
Ye keek at black an white then richest colour,

deith an decay then bonnie sichts.
Derkness neist tae captivatin beautie.

Mair nor subtitles needit tae mak sense o it.

Frontiers

Behind Beijing lay the monastery,
high on a hill at Badachu.

We climbed towards the blue sky,
watched Buddhist monks toil in
saffron robes, tend plants, herbs.

A song drifted,
rhymed with wind chimes,
curled its notes through
pink shrubs, buzzing insects,
fell away into the city smoke below.

We knew that tune,
'*Auld Lang Syne*', now '*Old Friends*'
in Mandarin.

Our homeland seemed so far while abroad,
but we'd glimpsed that harmony, unity,
that knows no frontiers.

Tian'anmen kites

Tak the Metro, he'd said, so,
lik mowdies,
we burrowed unner the city.

No a bat's in hell's chance
o readin the names.
Each stop a Chinese puzzle,
us trappt in wir Roman alphabet.

Mandarin tonals chattered
a chorus we couldnae ken,
keekt wee glances at wir
white faces, grey herr, roon een.
Ilka bit that different fae
wir fella stravaigers

Gan oot at Tian'anmen Square
we blinkt in the smoorie licht.
A muckle sea o reid brick laid oot
lik a welcoming cairpet.

Ayont the Square wir waas,
an the Gate o the Forbidden Citie,
an faur abuin it a michtie image
o Mao Zedong.

Aroon us, kites fleed lik sowels set free,
in shapes o eagles, dragons,
flown here bi adults an aw.
Fir here, lik puppetry in Eastern Europe,
this is a grown-up hobby,
Anither culture gap
we dinnae unnerstaun.

Kites an puppets
caught, trappt, manipulated.
Pouer an control
no able tae brak free.
Deid if they did.

At the Gate tae the Forbidden Citie
stood wir son, safe, healthy, free.
Bit trappt in wir memories,
tanks still rolled in echty-nine,
the student aw his lane mowed doon,
the ootrage warld-wide.

We couldnae yet accept wir son's adoptit hame.
Fir noo, we hugged him
unner the Mao Zedong image,
thocht o anither mither,
no able tae dae this,
never able tae dae this.
Reid kites soared
intae a blue lift.

Let's hear whit the dragon hud tae sey aboot the Olympics

Aw naw don't even ask me aboot thon
Well aw richt go aheid nae herm in askin
It's a free kintra weil that's no quite true it isnae free at aw
Naethin's free
Communist? Communist ye sey?
Ye huv tae pey fir scuils,
Ye huv tae pey fir doactors
Ye huv tae pey fur hoaspitals
There's nae pension
Nae nuthin fur nuthin
Aw sorry
A wee diversion thair
It wis the Olympics yes wir speirin aboot
Weel it's aw connectit up isn't it?
There's dosh fir a new metro,
Dosh tae build new ring roads roon Beijing
Dosh tae learn aw the taxi drivers hoo tae speak English
No tae gob
Dosh fir cleanin aw the beggars an down's syndrome folk aff
    the streets
Dosh fir sortin aw the roads an plants aw up the middle o toon
Paintin the grass green when the committee cam oot
Dosh fir biggin a new stadium
Ken mair nor wan new stadium
Thir's umpteen
Ye cannae muive fir migrant wurkers
Up fae the sticks tae bigg up the citie
Ye see thaim hingin aboot when thay're aff

Naethin tae dae an nae siller tae dae it
Knee deep in stoor and glaur aw day
An twintie tae a dormitorie aw nicht
It must be murder
A sometimes hink aboot thaim when a'm at ma telly in ma cave
Should mibbe invite thaim in o a nicht
We'd hae a bit in common ken
Me bein a rural bloke masel
Bit na, chairitie begins at hame they sey
A've goat the wee lassie roon the corner comin in
A'll be hivin her fir ma tea
A hid the mannie neist door for breakfast yisterday.
Aye Olympics. Ye'll hiv tae come back tae me oan that yin.

Mao's mangoes

In nineteen sixtyeight, Mao gave some workers
a gift of mangoes.

The fruit transformed overnight
into a sacred relic.

Wax, plastic, ceramic models followed
and mango-covered duvets,

mango posters,
mango-decorated enamel cups.

The thirty six real Mao mangoes were sent
on tour like pop stars to fanatical fans.

Mango facsimiles, believed to be original,
filled families with delight.

Now, in Mao's mausoleum,
his corpse shines like wax fruit.

Some say rot has set in.
A slice of ear has detached itself,

like an Autonomous region.
The body corrupting, breaking up.

Queues still form
in Tian'anmen Square to gaze upon it.

The fruits of his labours
linger on.

Pooling

Hunan traders
at Panjiayuan market
sell decorated bowls.

They're from
The Great Leap Forward,
'60s and '70s

when people pooled bowls
utensils, containers,
for communal events.

Nailprints engraved names
for easier retrieval,
though while dining, sharing,

each individual's thoughts
remained in solitary isolation,
prisoners in silent cells.

The market today is
noisy with old folk
in flowered pyjamas and

flat black canvas shoes,
retrieving memories
deep as bowls,

sharp as gauges on clay,
rare as collector's items.

The shard box

My son gifts me a carved wooden box,
its concave lid inset with porcelain.
Down in an eastern corner, tiny stars round its edges.

Fine line brush strokes depict a kimonoed woman,
black hair piled high, pale purple flowers curve round her clasp.

In the flag-red velvet interior a tiny paper tells,
The Story of the Shard Box.

During the Cultural Revolution, the keeping of treasures,
deemed bourgeois, was thus illegal.

Collectors broke their porcelain
    and threw it away.

Now, it's sought, pieced together as citizens repair treasures.

While porcelain and people shattered,
back then, we busied ourselves becoming a family,
    fragmented now

our young such a keen diaspora,
my own gone to that State which keeps its glue-like grip

on every corner of its empire
the way a mother can't, shouldn't.

If only a family too could be reconstructed,
dovetailed into what we once were.

'The Delights of Roaming Afar'
for *Christina Schmigel*

After the reading on the Bund,
the Pearl Tower distracting me through the venue's window,
the Shanghai studio took a bit of finding.

We wove our way through neon lit bars
calling in at that weird vegetarian restaurant
which serves meat-replica dishes.
Only the Chinese, masters of the counterfeit,
could disguise so perfectly.

You took me up several flights of stone stairs
passing cool looking artists on the way up.
The graffiti-covered walls were better
 than the average scribble
and bolted doors opened revealing
shocks of colour peeking
from studio interiors.

In this whirl we entered yours.
Living three years now in Shanghai
your work immersed and Asian influenced.

Here was a cabinet of eastern curiosities.
Little drawers lined with exquisite silk paper,
minute china teacups, scrolls of radical scripted paper,
moongates sat on the floor, mandarin characters hung from the
    ceiling.

In a corner, multi-coloured plastic baskets
awaited dismantling by your art student assistant.
Work-in-progress growing into
skyscrapers emulating a mini-Shanghai cityscape.

Beside your conceptual art,
words seemed too concrete.
But maybe your colours are my adjectives,
your fabrics my nouns,
your methodology my verbs.

NOTE
*'The Delights of Roaming Afar' is the title of an art installation originally
appearing in Shanghai. American artist Christina Schmigel took the title
from the work of Shen Fu (c.1806) who wrote 'Six Records of a Floating
Life'. He was a distinguished designer of gardens.*

35

Going East

At Suzhou, wrinkled women crouch on pavements,
lace silk thread through minute white balls.
Everyone is buying these rubber-looking bracelets.

Renminbi clink and chink
into pancake flat saucers.

In the *Tao Gardens of The Humble Administrator,*
The Master of the Nets, Tingfeng,

rain fills lotus leaves;
wax cups overflow into the lotus below,

down into the next, and the next,
making tiny fountains, trickling notes.

Under a cherry red bridge, a figure huddles,
collecting seeds or something from floating centres.

It's white balls of lotus seed, strung like pearls
an annual worship of the Buddha's flower.

Later, we too place *renminbi* in plates,
ring our wrists with little moon beads like rosaries,

feel tiny globes shift under our fingertips.
The East opening for us, that morning, like a flower.

Aw the Ts in China

Don't mention the three Ts,
A was telt;
Tian'anmen, Tibet, Taiwan.

So A didnae.
Bit A drank everythin in.

37

Lobbie

The Hexi Corridor,
kent as the craig o Cheenie,
gans west o the Yella River.
A lang neuk raxin oot
tae the Great Wa's last fort.

The auld ramshackle Silk Road
tae Central Asia, Persia, an oan tae Europe.
The new route 312s
fower lane highway
takks traffic intae the desert.

Twa ridd ens in this twa mindit kintra.
Yin an yang.
Citie folk an peasants.
Capitalists an Confuscionists.

An the West speirin, wunnerin whit wey
it micht gan oan the lang lobbie tae democracie.

Wan wean policie
for R.G.

There ur ower monie Cheenie folk,
says the government official,

as she trevells oot wi nurses
tae toons an villages.

Some wimmen jist weeks pregnant,
some echt month, nine month.

Watter bubbles an rocks in a bucket
whyles the breathin peters oot.

There ur ower monie Cheenie fowk,
she repeats her mantra.

Luiks surprist at the journalist's speirins,
muives oan wi her bucket.

There ur ower monie Cheenie folk.

Mei ban fa

you took our land
developed our fields
spent our money
we tried to complain
you sent in officials

there's nothing to be done
mei ban fa

the villagers ask
'how can we move forward?'
mei ban fa

you sent in the army
the peasants protested
you sent in the thugs
we tried to fight back
you sent in the guns

mei ban fa
mei ban fa

(*Mei ban fa: There's nothing can be done*)

Down pingjiang lu in Suzhou

Down pingjiang lu in Suzhou, renovation's rife.
Old buildings gutted out by the little canal.

Through an open paint-cracked door
we glimpse a musical instrument.

My Chinese companion tells me
it's the seven stringed *qin*,

A string for an element;
Gold, wood, water, fire, earth, and two Kings.

There are thirteen lunar dots, exotic as an eighth day
or a fifth season or this trip to south China.

Rosewood fragrances the air,
bamboo screens a practising student.

We leave the sanctuary,
drift like notes along the canal bank.

I think of bagpipes in our Piping school
in Glasgow's Cowcaddens.

The Clyde flowing the width
of ten wee canals.

How I've never blown a bagpipe,
drink whisky only as a hot toddie cure.

Can you play your national instrument? I ask,
Drink your national drink?

But you tell me you never learnt the *qin* at school,
don't like drinking *baijiu*.

We wander on, pluck memories like chords
from our respective nations.

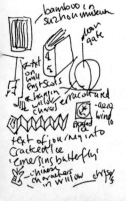

Crane

One pronounciation of China is
chai le, meaning *let's demolish*.

Time was when a crane
was a bird on a delicate painting
of peony or sharply pointed mountain.

Classic Chinese emblem,
symbol of an art form spanning centuries.
Tang, Chang, Ming.

Today, a different yellow crane hovers over the skyline,
dips to lift another crate of bricks.

Houses disappear overnight, hotels emerge
Beijing rebuilt before my eyes.

Facelifts and botox can leave a patient
devoid of a past, unable to smile.

New world constructed
from recycled courtyard hutongs,
replicated pagodas.

A nation counterfeits itself.

Pouring tea

A tea boy is pouring
from a long spout,
impossibly long,
into paper thin porcelain cups.

We're sure he'll spill
some blood red tea
on the skin coloured silk cloth.
But his hand is firm,
steady as a dictator.
Nothing distracts him from his task.
Everything is perfectly controlled.

Only at the end,
turning to leave,
his thick black pigtail
swishes like a clock's pendulum,
and the fragile china tremors.

cracked ice

christinas studio

a cabinet of
curiosities

Cracked Ice

Across China
there's fretworked wood
on shutters, doors and windows.

These lattice patterns are
unique as snowflakes,
one booklet states.

It's 'Cracked Ice' I'm hooked on,
recurring motif-like on an
Emperor's ancient dressing-room door,
then just as likely on a
state-of-the-art apartment's
frosted bathroom window.

Ice crystalises now
on this cabin's porthole
at high altitude over Russia.

A former State cracked open
into new sharp edged boundaries.
A model the People's Republic seems not to follow.

The plane loses height, touches down,
ice particles dissolve in the warmer atmosphere.

Fellow passengers, Chinese included,
crumple up their sachets
of Golden Hover Fish Fillets,
dried snack packets of Apple chips,
strain to see through cleared portholes,
what's ahead.

In Suzhou

In the new museum,
clean lines coat corridors.
Fish crowd a pond.
Light fills the central ceiling.
Lattices decorate windows
set in white plaster walls.
Purity is the keynote.

A contemporary exhibition
includes nudes. A first for here.
A willow-filled window to the back garden
looks like a framed photo,
startles a bird flying into the space,
stuns its gaze on the future.

In the old Tao gardens,
small courtyards mosaic through parks.
Butterflies, dragonflies and insects,
creatures of the locality
are stone images under our feet.

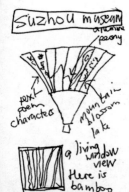

Ancient grey igneous rock bubbles in formations.
Pagodas house benches near darkened halls hung
with Tang and Song poem scrolls over
blackened wood furniture.
Tai chi is glimpsed behind some trees.
Goldfish swim through lily-ponded lakes,
deep orange hulks gliding just under
surfaces of slimed green water.
Permanent installations of
rain and sun, wind and moon.

Terracotta warrior

The visa was easy,
they let us in fine.
British Museum? They said.

No problem.
We will all keep together,
won't separate,
disperse across the country,
disappear like illegal immigrants

coming in in the back of a van,
no windows, no air,
darkness for three days.
Some don't make it.

Here we are,
all nicely wrapped,
carefully protected.

Even our air is first class in here.
Granted they don't need to feed us, but still,
we take some looking after.

Those poor sods in vans.
Half were dead on arrival,
the other half were half dead.

And anyway,
it's likely they'll drown themselves
picking illegal cockles
on a fog filled beach.

Yes, being a terracotta model is alright you know,
I can think of worse.
Though we were a long time coming,
and there's more of us waiting
beneath ground,
till the time is decreed,
the mercury reading right.

NOTE
a selection of the Chinese Terracotta Warriors was shipped to London in
2008 for a temporary exhibition.

Beijing spring

Ling Ling,
an MBA student, says she must choose
      another name.
Ling Ling says she must choose
      an English name.

Westerners can't pronounce our Chinese names,
      so we pick another.

Her own name sings like a bell.
      I tell her she should keep it.

We speed through ring roads and tolls,
      from airport, all steel and glass,
to hotel, all marble and wood.

Newness coats China like a spring outfit

I offer her my childhood name, Lizanne,
      If you must choose another, I say.

She thanks me, smiles politely,
      points out the opening peonies,
cranes rebuilding the city,
      billboards painted with Chinese characters and pinyin
      translations.

We try to discuss the naming of things,
      in our odd half languages.

      Later, her voice reverberates in my head.
I spend all night pronouncing it.

1001 Nights

Outside 1001 Nights
a white-haired man squats.
Beside him are his legs –
a wooden contraption on wheels.

Inside 1001 Nights
the meal is excellent;
traditional Turkish kebabs, sweet meats
culminating with coffee black as Aladdin's cave.

Perfect limbs bend and turn
as tassled-belly dancers sway,
to high pitched music.
White silk skinned belly buttons
are diamond studded.

When we were small
someone said, that if you used a screw driver
on a belly button,
your legs would fall off.

If this was a tale from Arabian Nights,
I'd do it, and, when
the perfect legs fall
onto the geometrical tiled floor
I'd run, fast as a fox,
offer them joyously to the man in the street.

Instead, we ask for the bill
and doggy bags,
hand the latter to the beggar outside,
wish for a genie in a teapot.

Fable

There's a point above the Gobi,
where you see lights glow.

It's Nomads lighting night fires,
horses tethered at tents,
motorbikes coated with dust,
exhausts silenced till morning.

Bunting will be swaying in the night breeze,
cheese curd tossed onto warm horses' milk,
patchwork, embroidered blankets
draped on floor beds.

We drove up from Beijing once,
stopping overnight in Zhangjiakou,
the University dormitories packed
ten students to a tiny room.
Bathroom floor flooded under cracked pipes.

Our taxi skidded to a halt,
sand clogging tyres.
The driver says his wife expects him home,
but he sleeps curled in his seat
till morning brings better travelling light.

We sleep in moon-white yurts filled with
double bed, television, decorated porcelain water basin.
Painted horses circle the lit canvas,
trapped like figures on an ancient urn

or passengers on a black night
in a homeward bound plane,
our trip already fading to a fable.

The great firewall

Like internet tourists,
young folk blog in wifi hutongs.

Can you hear it?
Keyboards clicking like tiny picks on stone.

Only a matter of time till
this virtual wall's knocked down.

Hacked-off citizens already
stonewall state blocks

less permanent than that other great wonder.

It's not Chinese whispers.
This Eastern world hammers to be heard.

Home

Old folk come around six of an evening
to small grass squares
under miniature pagodas.

They trail a white Pekinese
yapping after a plastic shuttlecock.

The whitehaired Chinese pensioners
bend limbs to kick, lob, catch
the shuttlecock dancing between them
like some tiny plane on a jerking flightpath.

NOTE
  'How often have you lain beneath rain on a stranger's roof think-
  ing of home'.

  WILLIAM FAULKNER

Hearin a sang fae ma boat

hearin a sang fae ma boat

whaur is this bonnie sang bein sung
    wi its wee an lang notes?

shore-win, saun-rain minglin wi the doule soun.

there's nae need tae hear it at the enns o the irth
    tae be gey deeply muivit.

a'm jist yin day away fae hame
    an it's brekkin ma hairt.

NOTE
owresett fae the Ming Dynasty Chinese o Chang Yu

Comet

Come back or lea forivver
dinna staun lik thon at the door
lik a stane statue
talkin aboot awthin atween us
wi a luik thit expects nae answer

in fact whit is herd tae imagine
isnae daurkness bit dawn
hoo lang will the leerie licht last
mibbe a comet will appear
trailin debris fae the ruins
an a list o failures
lettin them glitter, burn up an turn intae ash

come back an we'll bigg again wir hame
or lea forivver lik a comet
gliskin an cal lik frost
thrawin oot the daurk an sinkin back intae daurkness yince mair
gan throu the white lobby jynin twa nichts
in the glen whaur echoes arise oan aw sides
ye sing alane

NOTE
owresett fae the Chinese of Bei Dao

Boat ticket

he doesnae hae a boat ticket
hoo can he gan oan board
the rackle o the anchor chain
fashes the nicht here

the sea, the sea
the island that rises fae the ebbin tide
as lanely as a hairt
disnae hae the soft shadda o bushes
an lum reek
the mast that flashes
is struck intae fragments by lichtnin
coontless storms
hae left ahint fixed patterns
oan stieve scales an shells
an the wee umbrellas o jellyfish
an auld tale
is haunded oan by the ocean spray fae wave tae wave

he doesnae hae a boat ticket

the sea, the sea
the lichen tichtly massed oan the reef
spreids intill the nakit midnicht
alang seamaws' feathers gleamin in the daurk
an clings tae the screif o the muin
the drag has fawen silent
conch an mermaid stert tae sing

he doesnae hae a boat ticket

time hasnae come tae a stoap
in the clappit boat the fire is bein stoked
rekindlin reid coral flames
when the waves shouder up
glitterin an jinkin the een o the deid
float up fae the ocean depths

he doesnae hae a boat ticket

aye it maks ye deezie
the sunlicht dryin oot oan the beach
maks ye awfie deezie

he doesnae hae a boat ticket

NOTE
owresett fae the Chinese o Bei Dao

Stretch oot yer hauns tae me

streitch oot yer hauns tae me
dinna let the warld blokt bi ma shouder
fash ye onie langer
if luve is no forgotten
herdship lees nae mindin
mind whit A say
no awthin will pass
if there's anely wan last aspen
staunin big at the ridd en
lik a heidstane wi'oot an epitaph
the fawin leaves will speak an aw
fadin palin as they faw
slowly they freeze ower
haudin wir heavy fitprints
course naebodie kens the morra
the morra sterts anither dawn
when we'll be fast asleep

NOTE
owresett fae the Chinese o Bei Dao

Buttoning up

Here's a book says, *Clothes*
can send out messages.

The Qin warriors closed
their wraparound coats,
left side overlapping right.

The opposite showed
they were in mourning, or
turning your back on life.

I think of your wardrobe
still hung with jackets
she can't bring herself to fling out.

Harris Tweed for Sundays.
That light beige jerkin for summer,
making you look like other octogenarians,
fading into backgrounds,
dwindling out of things.

But you were always a
'straight-down-the-middle man'
buttons and zips, no nonsense.

Though, towards the end,
you'd have overlapped your coat
to the left,
if we'd let you.

Somebody else's Father's Day

An e-mail's come in from
Browse For Books
'Selected Books Dad will just love'

Even in his last years he didn't, couldn't;
not after two failed cornea implants,
or curtains of cloud-thick cataracts.

The pre-tuned radio helped for a while.
Talking Books, Talking Newspapers.
till his attention span shrunk
to the size of his living room window;
even that view petered out too.

The *Talking Watch* was handy,
as though that world of work still called.
Under his pillow, inside his pocket,
although going nowhere,
Time mattered.

The search was constant too
for the white stick lost
under chairs, tables, beds.

Rage never left him;
the eye operation botched,
'butchered', he'd say,
on a bad day,
his blue eyes fogged and faltering.

He peered through a mist,
as I do now, at this e-mail,
for Father's Day
for somebody else's.

Filing

After cutting his horn-like nails,
the grand daughter advised
daily filing.

So he sits,
an obsessive manicurist,
sawing back and forth
with a steel emery board.

Tired of the News,
what's new at eighty five?
He's filing down memories,
smoothing them into manageable pictures,
like a pebble in the Irish Sea
his forefathers crossed.

He sits below his picture
of the Vale of Avoca,
hears the banjo no longer strummed,
catches a tune on the silent harmonica
worries a stray regret from his youth.

Later, he'll dream of shamrock,
the Ring of Kerry,
Guinness in a long glass half empty;
the emery board dropped down the settee side,
lost like a life.

Sibling

Something was growing
inside our father.

No-one would name it.
Some called it a growth,

another a shadow.
This nurse says it's a mass.

Our Catholic upbringing
conjures up a ceremony,

behind the lung cavity.
Robes round ribs, hosts of hearts.

We want to believe
a transubstantiation is possible

Something was growing
inside our father.

Curled like a tiny foetus,
a wicked sibling,

a dark thing we tried to name,
a weird child's unwanted arrival.

If only it was a birthday,
we'd light candles, blow them out,

wish.

Life line

in the same way we as weans
wouldn't do as we were telt
now your own hand won't
something has happened
along the line of muscle and sinew
nerve and impulse
which channels information

something has happened
and your tea cup shakes like
a small home in an earthquake
its contents tip dangerously

we leap to your assistance
shift it to your good hand
feel eighty year old skin
stretch to fit the cup's curve

cellular baby cradle blanket
waffle peppered with square holes
your mind fretworked too
you try to leap the gullies
dark as this four am ward

the over hot hospital
is busy as the high street
you won't see again

something has happened
along the life line
which is fingering its end
palming our future without you
there's nothing we can throw you now
but our love
and a last goodbye

After the poetry workshops

On the last day, we held a showcase event,
for the new poems.

Photographs would be taken,
said a white-overalled science teacher.
Another insisted everyone must find a tie.

Girls rushed off to apply make up,
one boy added more hair gel.
Andrew added a line to his
'Questions without answers' poem after Neruda.
Why do girls always go to the toilet two at a time?
Everyone laughed at that line,
so mundane, but they knew by now that
poetry could be about anything.

Last redrafts, running orders, intros were written.

Suddenly Briony asked,
Can we write on the pink balloon?
We'd held a party the day before
for Nicole's fourteenth.
A birthday poised on the edge of childhood.
Let's write about freedom,
said Kevin.
So, everyone wrote on the balloon in black felt pen,
then read in turn,
Freedom is...
Letting go
A closed door about to be opened
Independence
and such like statements.

Scott stood, last in the line, beside the window
through which their balloon would be released.
He grasped it in his boy/man hands,
and turned to the window.
He pushed and pulled at the chrome catch,
his face flushing pink,
but school windows are locked
at smaller than balloon-sized gaps.

The young poets fell silent,
staring from balloon to window to boy.
The black word FREEDOM looked crumpled,
the balloon already starting to deflate.

Black Swan Moment with daughter

You sailed into the room with newspapers,
asked about the asterisk I'd inked against the phrase,
A Black Swan Moment.

I waxed eloquent for a while;
how Australian discoverers
thought all swans were white,
till they found black swans in their new land.

You left the room,
brought back, from your laden bookcase,
a thick hardback, just published;
The Black Swan Moment.

You agreed it was an amazing theory,
knew the philosophy that
one moment can alter
our thoughts, attitudes, lives.

I remember the two year old you,
talking incessantly;
watch you turn now,
return your book to its shelf,

glide out of the room,
towards the rest of your life.
I'd long suspected you might fly.

Photo reproduction by zvonko kracun

Efter ye cam back fae Malawi

Efter ye cam back fae Malawi,
A kent mair aboot thon muckle lan o
bens, lochs an singin folk,
the warm hairt o Africa.

A kent elephants jist see black an white,
thir is a derk side tae hippos,
that crocodiles wir gliskin by yer boat.

Wimmen cairry caur batteries
oan thir heids lik bunnets.
That muckle oan thir heids,
the world oan thir shouders.

A kent aboot the potter, dauncin by his table o pots.
Aids orphanage boays wi black smilin faces,
whae mimed an daunced,
Sang, *here we dig graves for our mothers,*
Bury her in the soil, sing her spirit to Heaven.

A kent aboot the scuil wi nae winnocks or lichts,
twa thoosan weans, an this rule fir the maisters
Arrive early, ye'll get a plastic chair,
arrive ower early an gaither leafs
tae redd oot the cludgies.

Efter ye cam back fae Malawi,
ye gied me widden bangles
carved intae lik the kintra ye'd seen
British, French, Belgian, Dutch.

Efter ye cam back fae Malawi,
the dry cleanin lassie said
aboot yer jaiket cuffs,
reid edged wi desert saun,
this'll mibbe be indelible.
An A kent she wis richt.

Efter ye cam back fae Malawi,
A wunnert, as we lay thegither
in wir clean bricht hame,
hoo much is a mishanter o birth.

Eatin locusts

Wance we'd seen Phnom Penn's Killin Riggs,
the bus shooglt throu Cambodia's kintraside
tae Siem's Reap's ancient temples.

Een oan stalks at hooses oan stilts,
shilpit widden shacks abuin broon glaur
thrang wi dugs, chickens, pigs.

Lik daithlie doylies,
thoosans o lanmines still lace the lan.

Fae the bus windae we seen
sheet efter sheet o white plastic,
strecht oan widden sticks lik a dream catcher
tae trap the nicht's fleein insects.

Stoppin fir a brekk oan the fower hoor journey,
we strecht wir legs, tuned wir lugs
tae rhythms an soons aroon us,
ettled tae droon oot the morn's horrors
an Pol Pot's legacie.

Merkets lined ridd ens, fowk piled fish, fowl, fruit,
ontae cloath covert trestle tables.

A lassie buys fae a platter heapt heich
wi shiny shapes bleck as nichtmares.
Herr tied perjink in a lacy bauble,
ye cuid see hingin fae her lugs
gowd earrins o pink lustre globes.

She hauns ower coins we dinna ken,
dip dips her reid paintit finnger nails
intae a paper poke, pulls oot bodie efter bodie,
brekks aff sherp claws, snaps aff pyntit heids,
chucks starin een oan tae the grun,
an pops locust efter locust atween her pink lips.

The loudspeaker tree

Phnom Penh,
an we've gan tae
the Killin Riggs.

The seventies, a raicent genocide,
an this kintra is ower puir
tae mak a monument,
sleek an smert.

Skulls pile high unner a plain gless front,
riggs undulate whaur deep pits haud bodies still.
A shin bane juts fae the grun,
rippt claes clothe the stanes.
A reid fragment flaps fae a brainch.

Oor guide loast mither, faither, brither,
in Pol Pot's regime.
He shaks his heid,
shaws us a palm tree's muckle leaves,
machete sherp, taks ma finger,
pits it douclie oan the spine.

Its pynts skyward lik a comb's teeth.
Here they slauchtered weans,
nae weapons needit,
whyles a loudspeaker droond oot
the noise o deein fowk.

Oor guide sets aff again
across the grun pitted an reuch.
We walk quate ahint his shadda.

Mindin

a'm washin glaur-steeped claes efter
simmer stravaigins
bangkok citie smoor
then north tae chiang rai's
jungle trek

noo it's midgies no mosquitoes
sausages no green bean stir fry
a'm peelie wallie white noo insteid o broon
an A mind the village tribes,
Aka, Lana, Karen.

woks smoke unner bamboo roofs
lik oor aul hielan hooses they've nae lums
bleck pigs shit
neist widden shacks
wannerin chickens peck fir grain

hame tae july's drookit lift
nae warmth tae speak o.

a'm mindin oan thae weans
haudin oot bananas
broon een sperklin
pearlie teeth gliskin
white as this porcelain sink

whaur watter birls, drains,
disappears wi memories
a'm ettlin tae catch
wi stanes an dreams
fawin oot o deep pooches.

Above water

We take a boat along the Mekong,
Cambodia's lifeline.

Thin wicker eel baskets
line the river edge.
Elephants wait at the tribal post where
snakes in boxes are offered,
Take your picture with a snake?
He curl round your shoulder.
Crumpled pictures of braver tourists
are shown as bait.

At the river's head the Mekong pours into
the Tonle Sap, the Great Lake.
Locals populate this river lined with
shacks and schools on stilts,
churches and libraries on stilts.

Underneath, farmed trout thrash,
below others, crocodiles' leather hides
seek afternoon sun.

Come the rainy season, banks disappear
as the lake rises from one to fourteen metres.
The Mekong reverses its flow,
moves folk further inland.

Into the Great Lake's deepest spot,
we watch two children manhandle a paint-flaked canoe,
green weeds curling round its base.

Locals stop to watch our tourist boat turn to leave.
We try to watch the children's boat till it's
a dark dot far out at sea.

The perfect soldier

'The landmine is eternally prepared to take victims. It is the perfect soldier.'

JODY WILLIAMS, 1997 Nobel peace prize winner and founding coordinator of the International Campaign to Ban Landmines

Aki Ra thinks he's thirty.
He's not sure.
Orphaned in Cambodia,
he was trained,
at five years old,
to lay landmines.
His tiny child fingers perfect
for the job.

Mine ordnance is good,
and if an orphan blows himself up,
who will care? said the Khmer Rouge,
with their sure supply of child soldiers.

Mines, mortars, rockets, claymores, grenades,
fill Aki Ra's garden;
weapons he's unearthed.

Outside his shack of bamboo and tin,
there's shovel, hammer, wrench,
his life now given up
to digging up
the strange seed he'd planted.

Yellow

Thais, on Mondays,
wear yellow shirts
to show respect
for their King.

Today the street's a golden sea of
Polo shirts with king's crest
badges on their chest.

Some wear yellow
all week. Even the young,
who have known.
his reign so briefly.

We rustle the Bangkok Post
in our dark cedarwood hotel,
read that *yesterday the King*
actually held his own umbrella
at the display.

and,

The King will be awarded for
his services to the poor.

The hotel fountain patters its silver liquid
on the tiled floor.
We contemplate ornate mosaics,
recall the concrete pavements of home
consider variations on colour and royalty.

Tribe

We reach at last the bamboo stick shack.
Flat wooden sheets laid across for flooring,
upright poles scaffold thin muslin-screened curtain walls.
Even food is wrapped, cooked, served
on bamboo leaf plates.
The mud ground tries to suck us in,
our feet now red lump clogged.

Black pigs wallow beneath shacks,
a pig shits and two brown mounds
steam on the path.
In seconds, four chickens arrive
to rake for grains.

Identical brown dogs wander, forage, collapse,
wait in hope at open doors.

Outside every shack a solar panel shines
a government's gift in lieu
of new housing.

A boy from the Karen tribe climbs up
to watch us clean mud from hands and faces,
then slug Angor beer,
golden as the treasure in the Ankar temples.

He looks at my son closely, then edges nearer.
Once we're all sitting,
he pulls at the black hairs
on my son's arms and legs
with his small dirt-ingrained fingers,
then sells us his drawings.

All night the rain forest circles the village,
mud flows under shacks.

We breathe together under a shared moon.

Back home
for B. and K. Morrison

Back in Scotland,
I'm driving to work and slow down
for cars stopped on the road.

A woman wraps something in a blanket.
Its tiny red face pokes out.
I think it's a fox, but,
it's a rare red panda,
escaped from a local zoo.

We saw these last month in Chengdu.
You who wrote of urban foxes,
Deptford Beast, Jack the Ripper.
Examined man's mind in its darkest moments.

We're all in a better place now,
as the cliché goes.
Except the red panda of course,
or that fleeting fox thought of words
still escaping down shady roads.

Chinglish mesostic

<pre>
                    K
                    E
                    E p
                    O ff the grass.
        Your care F ul step keeps tiny grass
                    invariably green.
Protect a piece of green leaF and dedicate a share of love.
          Show mercy T o
                  t H e slender
                  Grass.
          I like you R smile but unlike your shoes
          on my f A ce.
          Dedicate a S hare of love.
          Green gras S dreading your feet.
</pre>

Postscripts

Dialogue with Daughter

We're busy google mailing between Scotland and Beijing.
I tell you my new book will be titled, *The Shard Box*.
You tell me it's a lovely name,
list all the things it makes you think of:

small secret things
pieces of other things
pieces of personal momentos
maybe remnants of fabric that are linked to particular people,
    times, memories
also tinder box, which makes me think of ballet and children's
    stories and also real coal fires
and also the cafe on byres road where i sometimes used to go
shards of mirror too, so reflection and self-reflexive-ness (is that
    a word?)
shards of mirror = lots of different perspectives

I say, all in all, I think it connects to central idea of elements being
made whole, what can be collected up, what can be repaired?

You say, *repaired suggests jumping off point – is something*
    damaged?
Is that the case?

I answer, all our lives is a breaking up and renewing of cells, finding
or failing in relationships, or nations which come and go in terms
of governments, unity then diversity and often damage to lives.

There is all around us damage and if things go well, repair...
maybe all humans want everything repaired.

You tell me, *that makes me a bit sad that you see it that way
round*

I reply, no not sad just realistic.

You try to convince me, *I like to try and think we are in a state
of always production, things growing, and damaged suggests it
was once perfect and now isn't.*

I can only say, maybe it's an older age thing? Growing is what
younger people do?
Don't be sad.

You countermand with, *but things were never perfect, we all work
with the things we have and humans are a bumpy lot and that's
where the diversity and mystery and opportunities and creativity
all come from.*

I sign off then. Imagine you returning to that life so different from
my own. An 8 hour time difference but worlds apart.

'*He expressed particular enthusiasm with respect to visiting the wall of China. I caught it for a moment, and said I really believed I should go and see the wall of China had I not children... 'Sir', (said he), by doing so you would do what would be of importance in raising your children to eminence. There would be a luster reflected upon them from your spirit and curiosity. They would be at all times regarded as the children of a man who had gone to view the wall of China. I am serious, Sir'.*
Boswell's *A Life of Johnson.*

Postscript 2

Two of my children live in Beijing. It has been their 'spirit and curiosity' that led me to travel to the east. A reverse scenario from Johnson's. I admire their ability to cope admirably with those days known to residents as a 'China day' – a euphemism for times when things get tough. Their philosophy of 'engagement' with this complex, controversial nation has opened up opportunities for many people, Chinese and others, in the pages of books and on the football field.

My son has been resident in Beijing since 1999 and co-owns China Club Football Ltd. – a blending of his lifelong favourite pursuits, football and languages, and a magnet for residents and visitors interested in football leagues and charity sponsorships matches and a host of fitba-related pursuits. Further information available at:

www.clubfootball.com.cn or **www.wanguoqunxing.com**

My daughter was Festival and Programmes Director for four years with The Bookworm, Beijing, responsible for selecting and managing the authors coming to read and take part in literary discussions. There are also Bookworms in Suzhou and Chengdhu and all branches run a rich cultural programme maintained throughout the year with a March International Literary Festival highlight. Alex Pearson, Pete Gough and Jenny Niven have created a cultural hotspot which is a must for anyone visiting these cities. Further information available at:

www.chinabookworm.com

(Jenny has now flitted to Melbourne where she is the Programme Manager for the Melbourne Writers' Festival.)